A New Home for a

A play by Ronda Armitage
Based on the original picture book
Illustrated by Holly Swain

Characters

Jed

Mum

Pirate 3

Narrator 1

Bird

Pirate 4

Narrator 2

Old Dog

Pirate 5

Pirate chorus

Sheep

Pirate 6

Ted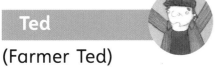
(Farmer Ted)

Pirate 1

Pirate 7

Dad

Pirate 2

Red Bull

Scene 1

On board a pirate ship

Pirate-style music is playing. Mum and Dad are dancing with the pirate chorus. Jed is standing to one side, looking out to sea. The dancers pause when the narrators walk in.

Narrator 1: Jed was a pirate, but he didn't enjoy it. He didn't like the way the ship kept bobbing about.

Dad:	Ahoy, Jed!
Mum:	Come and join our pirate dance!
Pirate chorus:	Oo-aarrgh, Jed! Come and sing our pirate song with us!
Jed:	I think I'd rather listen ...

Pirate chorus:

We're wibbly-wobbly pirates with wibbly-wobbly knees,
We're the wibbly-wobbly terrors of the wibbly-wobbly seas.

We've got wibbly-wobbly cutlasses and wibbly-wobbly parrots,
And when it's time for dinner, the parrots eat our carrots.

We like to shout 'OO-ARGH!' and
climb the wibbly-wobbly rigging,
And when the music plays, we all do
wibbly-wobbly jigging!

Narrator 2: Every day, Jed was seasick. Every night, Jed dreamt of a house that stood still.

Narrator 1: One day, Jed had something important to say.

Jed: Mum, Dad – I'm leaving.
I want a house that stands still,
with a view from a hill
and a roof that's blue like the sky.
And when I've found it, you can all come to stay.

Pirate chorus: Oh no-ho-ho-ho-ho! Jed's leaving!

Dad: Shiver me timbers!

Mum:	What a shock! But we can see you've made up your mind, lad.
Dad:	Aye, and when you've found your house, we'd love to come and visit.

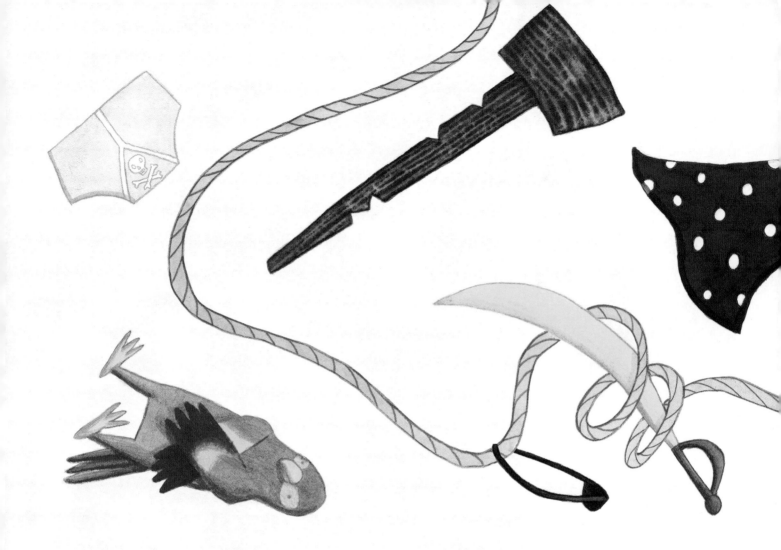

| Narrator 1: | Mum, Dad and the other pirates helped Jed to pack all his pirate things in an old trunk. |

| Pirate chorus: | Here we go-ho-ho! |

Mum, Dad and the pirate chorus take turns to run on stage, each carrying something to put into Jed's pirate trunk.

| Mum: | One long rope ... |

| Dad: | One pirate hat ... |

| Pirate 1: | Clean underpants ... |

| Pirate 2: | Your great-grandad's wooden leg ... |

| Pirate 3: | One spotted handkerchief ... |

Pirate 4:	A cutlass ...
Pirate 5:	One parrot (stuffed) ...
Pirate 6:	An eye patch ...
Pirate 7:	A clean pair of socks ...
Mum:	Your pyjamas ...
Dad:	And a toothbrush.
Jed:	Cheerio-ho-ho everybody! See you soon!
Pirate chorus:	Cheerio-ho-ho, Jed!

Scene 2

On land

Jed put his trunk on the back of his bike and cycled away.

Jed cycles through the countryside.

After a while, he came to a forest. A bird was squawking.

Bird: Please can you help? My nest is a mess!

Jed: Shiver me timbers! I've got the very thing. Your nest will fit perfectly inside this pirate hat!

Bird: Thank you! You're very kind – for a pirate!

Jed: I'm not a pirate any more. I'm looking for a new home.
I want a house that stands still, with a view from a hill
and a roof that's blue like the sky.

Bird: Will there be a tree?

Jed: Of course! Come with me. We'll look for a new home together.

Narrator 1:	After a while, they came to a field. A sheep was baa-ing loudly.
Sheep:	Baa, baa! Please can you help? I'm all tangled in brambles.
Jed:	Shiver me timbers! I've got the very thing. I can use my cutlass to set you free!

Sheep: Oh, thank you! You're very kind – for a pirate!

Jed: I'm not a pirate any more. I'm looking for a new home.
I want a house that stands still, with a view from a hill
and a roof that's blue like the sky.
With a stretching-high tree.

Sheep: Will there be a grassy field?

Jed: Of course! Come with us. We'll look for a new home together.

Narrator 2:	They came to a high bank. An old dog lay whimpering.
Old Dog:	Please can you help? I've broken my leg.
Jed:	Shiver me timbers! I've got the very thing – my great-grandad's old wooden leg! I'll tie it on with this spotted handkerchief. That will keep your leg straight till it mends.

Old Dog: Oh, thank you! You're very kind - for a pirate!

Jed: I'm not a pirate any more. I'm looking for a new home.
I want a house that stands still,
with a view from a hill
and a roof that's blue like the sky.
With a stretching-high tree
in a field (bramble-free).

Old Dog: Will there be a doormat?

Jed: Of course! Come with us. We'll look for a new home together.

Narrator 2: They came to an open gate. A red bull was bellowing at them.

Red Bull: I want to chase you!

Jed: Shiver me timbers! Luckily, I've got the very thing.

Narrator 1: Jed took out the rope and pulled his bike up into a tree. Farmer Ted came running.

Ted:	Shoo! Shoo!
Narrator 2:	He chased Red Bull back into the field.
Jed:	Thank you! You're very kind – for a farmer!

Ted: Oh dear! I'm not really a farmer any more. There's only Red Bull and me. I'd rather be a pirate. Yes, that's the life for me - on a rollicking, rolling ship, on a rollicking, rolling sea.

Jed: Oh dear! I'm not really a pirate any more. My friends and I are looking for a new home, too. We want a house that stands still, with a view from a hill and a roof that's blue like the sky. With a stretching-high tree in a field (bramble-free) and a doormat where Old Dog can lie.

Ted:	Come with me. I think I've got the very thing.
Narrator 1:	Farmer Ted took them over to the hill.
Ted:	Are you looking for a house like mine?
Jed:	Yes, it's perfect!

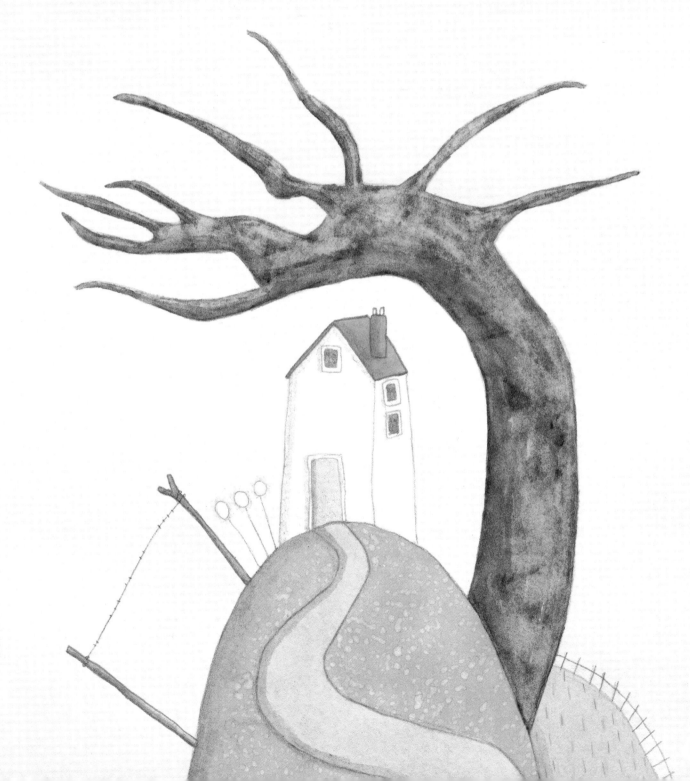

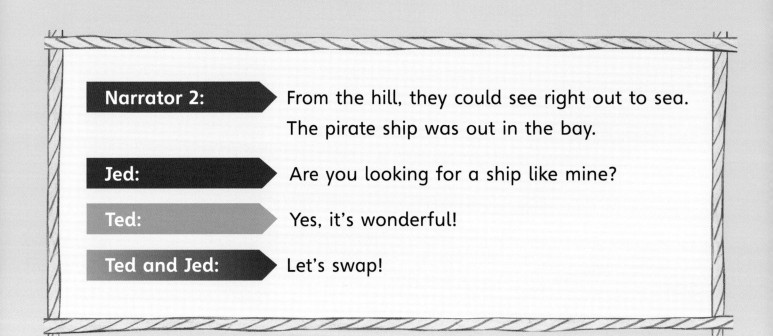

Narrator 2: From the hill, they could see right out to sea. The pirate ship was out in the bay.

Jed: Are you looking for a ship like mine?

Ted: Yes, it's wonderful!

Ted and Jed: Let's swap!

Scene 3

Back on the pirate ship again

Narrator 1:	Jed introduced Ted to his family.
Jed:	Ted wants to be a pirate. Can you help?
Pirate chorus:	Oo-aarrgh! Of course we can!
Dad:	We'll show 'im how to be a pirate!
Mum:	We're the best pirate teachers in the world!

Narrator 2:	Ted passed all the pirate tests.
Pirate 1:	Pirate talk ...
Pirate 2:	Reading a treasure map ...
Pirate 3:	Gangplank walking ...
Pirate 4:	Cutlass class ...
Pirate 5:	Spelling pirate words ...
Pirate 6:	Looking after parrots ...
Pirate 7:	Singing pirate songs ...

Narrator 1:	The pirates were so impressed that they invited him to join their plucky crew immediately.
Pirate chorus:	Oo-aarrgh, Ted, you're not bad for a landlubber!
Ted:	Oo-aarrgh, me hearties!
Narrator 2:	Ted liked his new home.
Ted:	Oo-aarrgh! This is the life for me. On a rollicking, rolling ship, on a rollicking, rolling sea. Cheerio-ho-ho, me hearties.
Pirate chorus:	Cheerio-ho-ho-ho-ho!
Narrator 1:	And Jed knew Ted would make a great pirate indeed!

Narrator 2: Jed liked his new home, too. Bird sang in the tree. Sheep munched in the field. And Old Dog slept on the doormat.

Jed: I've a house that stands still, with a view from a hill and a roof that's blue like the sky. A perfect new home for a pirate.

Red Bull: Moo!

Everyone sings the pirate song again.